Ocean Breeze Books
Los Angeles, California

Edgar Hernandez

My Story

*Proceeds from this book will be donated to
The General Alfred Valenzuela Family Foundation.
More info on back.*

Edgar Hernandez: POW - An American Hero
Publisher & Contributor: Alfredo Perez
Ocean Breeze Books
964 E. Badillo Ave. Suite 238
Covina, CA 91724
OceanBreezeBooks@yahoo.com

For information on other titles visit us at:
HonoringForgottenHeroes.com

Library Of Congress Control Number: 2008931144

Cataloged as follows:
1. Biography
2. Military History

ISBN: 978-0-9818934-0-2

Cover Photos:
1) In the deserts near the Southern Iraqi City of Nasiriyah,
Monday, March 2003. (AP Images/Itsuo Inouye)
2) Image from video seen on Iraqi television of captured
American soldier being interviewed Sunday, March 23, 2003.
He was identified by family as Edgar Hernandez of Texas.
(AP Images/IraqiTV Via APTN)

Distributed by: Atlas Books
Photos courtesy of friends of Edgar Hernandez
Cover & layout design: Alfredo Perez

Edgar Hernandez

POW

An American Hero

Written by Jose Martinez
& Megan Rellahan

Ocean Breeze Books
Los Angeles, California

This book is dedicated to the memory of
Private Ruben Estrella-Soto,
Edgar's best friend killed in combat on
March 23, 2003 in Nasiriyah, Iraq,
as well as his friends and fellow soldiers
who died that bloody day.

This book is also dedicated to Edgar's father,
José Refugio Hernandez, who passed away
due to a severe stroke.

Private Ruben Estrella-Soto
April 22, 1984 – March 23, 2003
Pictured here with parents Ruben Sr. and Amalia

In Beloved Memory of
Jose Refugio Hernandez
July 4, 1945 – September 29, 2007
Pictured here with family

These brave heroes were killed in the ambush at
Nasiriyah, Iraq on March 23, 2003:

Chief Warrant Officer Johnny Villareal Mata, El Paso, Texas

First Sergeant Robert J. Dowdy, Cleveland, Ohio

Staff Sergeant George Edward Buggs, Barnwell, S. Carolina

Sergeant Donald R. Walters, Kansas City, Missouri

Specialist Jamaal R. Addison, Roswell, Georgia

Specialist Edward J. Anguiano, Brownsville, Texas

Specialist James M. Kiehl, Des Moines, Iowa

Private First Class Howard Johnson II, Mobile, Alabama

Private First Class Lori Piestewa, Tuba City, Arizona

Private First Class Brandon U. Sloan, Bedford, Ohio

Private Ruben Estrella Soto, El Paso, Texas

Contents

Contents

An American Hero

Chapter One

The Morning of the Bloody Battle

In the dead of night in the Iraq desert of Nasiriyah, three days into Operation Iraqi Freedom, seven U.S. soldiers gathered together, joking with one another. Sadly, only two of those soldiers would ever return home.

"People were talking about dying," remembered U.S. Army Specialist Edgar Hernandez, age 21. "Some of those same people who talked about dying were killed in combat."

Private Brandon U. Sloan, age 19, was one of those who never made it Stateside again. "Sloan told me we are all going to die," Hernandez recalled. "He called his mom from Kuwait and told her the same thing."

To help lighten the mood, Hernandez and Sloan decided to "mess with" a sleeping buddy, rubbing a piece of grass under his nose, waiting for a reaction.

Later, back in his truck eating an enchilada MRE (Meals Ready-to-Eat), a delicacy and a reminder of home for the soldiers, Hernandez was joined by his best friend, Private Ruben Estrella-Soto, age 18. Desperate for an enchilada MRE of his own, Estrella tore the back of the truck apart in vain while the two buddies talked about the impending battle.

"Did you hear about the unit that was ambushed?" Estrella asked. "What if that happens to us?"

"Don't worry," Hernandez retorted. "We're going to be OK."

Dropping any kind of brave front, Estrella confessed, "I'm scared, Dude."

Later that night, March 22, 2003, a convoy of military vehicles took off, continuing its journey to Baghdad. Stopping to refuel, Hernandez pulled security duty. "Every time we stopped, we had to secure the area," Hernandez explained. "We grabbed our weapons and layed on the ground. On that night you could see all the explosions in the distance. And I said to myself, 'lots of people are dying right now,' and it felt weird. There were Iraqis dying but we were safe. I wasn't scared, just nervous."

A group of 18 trucks not certain of their exact position made up the convoy. Driving down Highway 8, code-name Route Blue, the soldiers could see the city lights as they approached a fork in the road. Now deserted, the terrain was earlier manned by U.S. troops to guide soldiers in the right direction. Without assistance, the convoy went the wrong way.

Hernandez noticed his commander, Captain Troy Kent King, age 37, talking to Marines, "maybe asking for directions," he guessed. As it turned out, those Marines would be part of a dramatic battle to secure Nasiriyah.

Soon enough, Hernandez saw a very odd sight. "We suddenly were passing a U.S. Marine battalion of tanks. They looked pretty cool. So, now some of us started asking, 'Why are we passing these tanks?' I never questioned that. To me, I thought they were just there.

"We were driving toward the city and could see the lights getting closer. We stopped a couple of times and pulled security. Not everyone in our group, including me, had radios so we just followed the convoy. The commander was calling headquarters for directions and we started getting scared. Those who had radios knew we were lost because they could hear the conversations."

On the morning of March 23, 2003, the convoy approached the city of Nasiriyah. Close to 5AM, the countryside was very quiet with the exception of barking dogs. Driving underneath the bright blue sun, the convoy passed a military checkpoint.

"These were Iraqi guards and they had AK-47 assault rifles. They were waving at us," Hernandez recalled. "This was weird. This was the enemy and here we were passing them. Some of us thought they had surrendered. This is still puzzling because it looked like we were lost. We crossed a bridge over the Euphrates River. There were ditches along the side of the road. We passed rice patties and the Saddam Canal. It turned from desert to green. There were palm trees everywhere. I told my shotgun driver Specialist Shoshana Johnson (age 32), 'This place looks like Vietnam. It no longer looks like the desert. It looks like a jungle.'"

Chapter Two

First Shots Fired

With most of the convoy trucks in need of gas and the group's tanker empty, it was apparent the soldiers were lost.

"I went to check the tank and Estrella, who was pulling security, helped me," Hernandez explained. "I found a stick and stuck it down my tank and realized I was very low on gas. I was getting nervous at that point. I remember seeing Iraqi men walking and others in vehicles passing by. I noticed they were on cell phones, and it turned out they were calling to plan the ambush."

All of a sudden, First Sergeant Anthony Pierce, age 31, came down along the convoy telling everyone to "lock and load!" Only those with radios knew the convoy was in enemy territory and about to be attacked.

Oblivious to the peril that surrounded him, Hernandez was busy taking pictures. "I noticed the sun was coming out and it looked very cool. As we jumped in our vehicles and started driving along the road, some Iraqi soldiers walked by with AK-47 assault rifles. One tried to hide his weapon and I asked Johnson, 'Look, did you see that?' I was getting really worried."

Driving a big rig and unable to move fast, Hernandez couldn't help but notice that the commander started picking up speed in his Humvee.

"That's when the back of our convoy started taking fire," Hernandez recalled vividly. "And that's when the First Sergeant in the rear of the convoy called the commander in the front and told him they were taking fire. Things picked up dramatically. The command was given for everyone to move. I saw everyone taking off and I said to myself, 'They are leaving us behind.' I started driving down the road really fast. We came to another intersection and made another U-turn. Those in the front of the convoy had made this U-turn and were gone."

Some, unfortunately, missed that turn and were left behind.

"I was trying to figure out what was going on,"

Hernandez pointed out. "Without a radio, I never heard the gunfire and did not know we were being attacked. Before making the U-turn, I saw Estrella and other soldiers stuck. The sides of the roads were muddy because it had rained the night before. I was saying to myself, 'Come on guys, let's go.'"

"Go around them!" Johnson shrieked.

Hernandez drove around the vehicles and could see through his rearview mirror other trucks stuck, as well.

"We saw a vehicle pull over with a lot of Iraqi soldiers in it," Hernandez declared, "and I drove off really fast. They got out and started shooting machine guns at the Army vehicles stuck behind me. Luckily, Estrella got out of the mud but there were others who didn't and died."

Chapter Three

The Firefight

Everyone was scrambling to get out of harm's way. Private First Class Lori Piestewa, age 22, and First Sergeant Robert Dowdy, age 38 stopped to pick up Private First Class Jessica Lynch, age 19, as well as Sergeant George Buggs, age 31, and Specialist Edward Anguiano, age 24, from 3rd Infantry Division.

"Their vehicle had too many people at this point and Lynch was in the truck bed of that Humvee with the other two soldiers," Hernandez said. "I was told later that

Sloan's truck was getting fired on while stuck in the sand. Sergeant Donald R. Walters was killed there while trying to escape the barrage of bullets. Sloan jumped in a vehicle with Private First Class Patrick Miller and Sergeant James Riley and they sped off. They were getting shot at and the bullets where flying everywhere, bouncing off their vehicles. Miller told me they were making that U-turn and he saw Sloan shaking. He had been shot in the head and was dying in the vehicle. Blood was pouring out from his forehead.

"I was racing down a four-lane highway driving past morning traffic. I was honking and getting fired on by AK-47s and we were receiving RPG fire from everywhere. I could hear the bullets bouncing off our vehicle. Then a dump truck got in front of me and would not let me pass. Iraqi soldiers with AK-47s kept popping out, shooting at us and I panicked. That's when I hit the brakes really hard and we almost got killed in an accident."

Hernandez and Johnson found themselves stuck halfway down an embankment, jackknifed. All of the remaining convoy trucks were passing them by still taking fire from every direction as Johnson was yelling, "Let's go! Let's go!"

"I saw three vehicles pass me," Hernandez recounted. "I saw Estrella pass me. He looked at me and yelled, 'Lets go!'"

Estrella, who had driven past, headed toward the Euphrates River Bridge and ran into an Iraqi tank and was killed instantly.

Within moments, Hernandez's truck was violently struck by an American Humvee. The soldiers inside appeared to be dead.

"I did not know who the driver was until I saw her," Hernandez recalled. "It was Piestewa. Her face was smashed and her leg was pointed in another direction. It looked terrible and I was freaking out. This was the first time I had seen dead people. I told Johnson they all died in the Humvee. I could see three bodies.

"But then I noticed Piestewa was still moving," Hernandez continued. "I could see her head and I wanted to go help her but I was scared I would get shot. I remember the second time I looked through the mirror she had stopped moving. Later, I found out that Piestewa died at the Tykar Iraqi Military Hospital."

There were three soldiers in the back of the Humvee. Two were thrown out and a total of four were killed. Only Jessica Lynch survived.

"We started panicking," Hernandez recounted. "Bullets were coming from everywhere. I looked back and saw Miller. Johnson was yelling for him to get down. And he said, 'No! They are chasing me.' I could see his face; it was very pale. He was scared. He said, 'I have to go, the Iraqis are coming after me,' and he kept running.

"That's when I said, 'Oh my God, they are coming,' and started scrambling for bullets and my weapons. I wanted to get all my magazines but some were stuck. Then Riley opened Johnson's door and said, 'Get out! Get out!' A bullet hit the door when I jumped out and fell face first in a ditch."

Hernandez, out of his vehicle and on the ground, hid under the truck for cover. He could see Johnson's legs sticking out from underneath and could hear RPG and gunfire as a grenade came rolling by. Fortunately, it did not explode.

Hernandez, feeling Johnson was in danger, rushed to her aid. Crawling towards one another, Hernandez reached out and grabbed a hold of her arm, attempting to pull Johnson to safety while the firefight escalated.

"I could hear the bullets fly by my head," Hernandez recounted. "I tried to quickly get back underneath my truck."

At that moment, partially exposed from under the vehicle, Johnson was shot in the ankles.

"I got hit! I got hit!" she screamed.

As the truck's tires were riddled with bullets, Hernandez tried to move away and was shot in the arm. "I looked down and saw blood gushing," Hernandez recalled. "The bullet must have gone right through."

Ducking grenades and machine gun fire, Hernandez knew the truck was ready to explode. "I could see the engine compartment and it was taking direct hits from bullets," Hernandez stated.

Minutes later, a second grenade was launched toward Hernandez, exploding just yards away with a loud "boom." Shrapnel struck him in the side of the face, knocking his helmet backwards.

"I panicked when I saw blood coming down my face and I told Riley I got shot in the head."

"No, no, no, stay down," barked Riley. "It's shrapnel, it's shrapnel."

Riley was in the prone position and the Iraqis kept shooting with everything; mortar fire and RPGs.

Unable to fire back and under intense attack due to the sand and dirt, all of their weapons were jamming.

"We didn't have time to clean our weapons because we were driving all the time," Hernandez opined. "I was bleeding all over. I thought I was never going to make it back home.

"I'm going to die, I'm going to die," Hernandez shouted in a panic.

"Shut up!" Riley ordered. "Don't say that!'

"I felt really scared but I didn't feel any pain," Hernandez remembered. "I was just holding my arm to stop the bleeding and that's when all the fear came into me. I started remembering my family and how they were going to have to bury me. I was thinking about my mom and how she's going to be crying at my funeral. I was thinking I am never going to get married and have kids."

Chapter Four

To Surrender or Die?

Filled with fear, Hernandez watched as swarms of people began circling the truck. Hidden underneath, Riley and his crew were out of options. Thoughts of death haunted Hernandez, and as a last attempt to protect his soldiers, Riley came out from under the truck and put down his weapon.

"We give up," Riley declared. "We surrender."

Wearing eyeglasses, Hernandez recalled witnessing an

Iraqi rip them off of Riley's face and start to punch him, repeatedly.

"I was sadly watching Riley getting hit and that's when another guy saw me," Hernandez said. "He came around the truck and pulled me up by my pants to look at him.

"As I was pulled towards Riley, we were both being punched. I was trying to hold my arm in order to stop the bleeding."

Still on the ground, a wounded Johnson told Hernandez later that she, too, was getting hit until they realized she was a female and stopped. With multiple blows to the face, Hernandez said, "There were like 30 or 40 people around us."

While some were Iraqi soldiers in green uniforms, others were pedestrians "running errands" and even young teenagers witnessed their attack.

"I also saw the Fedayeen (resistant fighters loyal to Saddam Hussein) wearing all black," remembered Hernandez. "They looked like ninjas with their faces covered and all you could see were their eyes. They all held AK-47s with their magazines across their chest."

As Hernandez's blurred vision began to clear, he noticed that it wasn't just the soldiers and Fedayeen who held weapons. Even the civilians were carrying AK-47s and while Hernandez continued to get hit, someone snatched his dog-tags and ran off.

"I turned around and looked back at my truck," Hernandez stated. "They were looting through all of our things and I could see them taking my CD player, my clothes, everything."

Hernandez watched as all the vehicles were ransacked. Feeling like a rope in a cruel game of tug of war, this young American hero was being pulled by both the Fedayeen and the Iraqi soldiers until one combatant came running towards them, shouting and carrying on.

"He must have given the Fedayeen an order to release us because they freaked, backing off as the Iraqi soldiers took us away," Hernandez pointed out.

Referring to the Fedayeen as "the crazy ones," Hernandez noticed that while the men in black wanted them dead, the Iraqi soldiers possibly had other plans for the Americans.

Hernandez was now a prisoner of war. Would he live or would he die? That was a question that neither he nor his fellow soldiers had the answer to and for the first time, they were faced with the possibility that in any given second, their lives could be over. Dreams of a future were put on hold and Hernandez just prayed that he could stay alive for one more hour.

Chapter Five

The World is Watching

Soaked in blood, Hernandez was growing weak and not passing out became a great challenge as this young soldier stood amongst his wounded peers while the Iraqis whispered to one another. While being placed in a truck, Hernandez saw Miller, whom he had witnessed running past him earlier. Obviously, he had been captured. It had become painfully clear that there was nowhere to run.

"We were their enemy," Hernandez thought. "And we are the only American soldiers here. We were losing hope. It felt like it was the three of us against all of them."

The whispering amongst Iraqi soldiers came to a halt and along with the just captured Americans, Hernandez was taken out of the truck and placed into another vehicle with two drivers who chatted with some of the rowdy pedestrians swarming the car. Hernandez's heart sank as the ecstatic Iraqi people danced and cheered in the streets.

"We didn't speak the language so we couldn't understand what they were saying except for the word 'American,'" Hernandez explained. "Women covered from head-to toe-danced while shrieking with glee."

Hernandez was taken to a compound where he staggered past a dirt patio and into an old building with "L-shaped rooms." The white tiled floors, walls with chipped paint and metal doors created a cold and dreary atmosphere. Walking through a room with a table and chairs, Hernandez saw Specialist Joseph Hudson, a member of the 507th, sitting by himself.

"He just looked at me with a blank stare," remembered Hernandez. "Later on, he told me that he was surprised to see me because he thought that he was the only one who survived."

Hernandez recalled Hudson saying, "Dude, when I saw you earlier, I thought you were going to die."

Shot in the back, Hudson didn't realize it until he felt the blood. Luckily, the Iraqi soldiers tended to his wounds; however, his partner Chief Warrant Officer Johnny

Villareal Mata wasn't as fortunate as a Nissan truck pulled next to Hudson and started firing with a machine gun through the metal door of the American vehicle.

"Mata was firing back at the Iraqis through Hudson's window and then they moved to his side of the truck," repeated Hernandez. "Hudson told me that he must have been shot already. His last words were, 'Please open the door' and then he died.

"Someone opened the door for Hudson and dragged his body out onto the ground. He said that when he opened his eyes, a bunch of Iraqis were pointing their weapons at him."

After being ordered to wipe the blood from his face, Hernandez was escorted into a room with a couch where he laid down. As a doctor was rushed in to stop the bleeding, Hernandez glanced at bar-covered windows. With an IV inserted into his arm, Hernandez's body began shaking, uncontrollably.

"I was just so tired and I wanted to go to sleep," Hernandez pointed out, "but the doctor kept talking to me in English."

Hernandez thought to himself, "I am going to bleed to death." As his friends watched in worry, Hernandez kept coming in and out of consciousness. He could hear faint voices as Iraqi soldiers questioned his peers and when he opened his eyes, a camera was pointing down at him.

"Only minutes from our capture," Hernandez said, "I was

dazed and as they lifted my head up for the camera, I realized they must have had me wash my face because they didn't want people to see me covered in blood.

"Looking back at that footage makes me laugh at myself because when they asked me where I am from, rather than give my name, rank, and serial number, I replied, 'Texas.'

"I just wasn't thinking right."

While Iraqi soldiers rummaged through all of their belongings, one by one, Hudson, Miller, Riley, Johnson and Hernandez were questioned. Without revealing any information, Hernandez followed the examples of Miller and Hudson and pretended that he was "confused" by what they were asking.

"The Iraqi officers started questioning us," remembered Hernandez. "When we told them we came from Camp Virginia, and that we had gotten lost, they didn't seem to understand what lost meant."

"What?" replied an Iraqi officer.

Miller responded by stating that they were trying to go to Baghdad and took a wrong turn. Realizing that the American soldiers weren't the main force, Hernandez said that they began thinking he and his peers were infantry.

"Where is the 82nd Airborne?" asked the Iraqi officers.

"101st Airborne?" they continued.

"We don't know," Hernandez and his friends responded.

The interrogators were asking questions very loudly but they were not being forceful.

Playing dumb, the group kept quiet. After Johnson was questioned, Hernandez watched the Iraqi soldiers help her walk by holding her shoulders.

"Blood was running down from her ankles and I could see the pain on her face," Hernandez stated.

All together in a cramped room, Hernandez said that Iraqi soldiers surrounded them while some peered through the windows from the outside, looking in.

"I remember there were a lot of Iraqi soldiers looking at us through the windows," Hernandez said. "I saw one guy's face and noticed that he was about my age. I remember thinking, 'That's my enemy. I'm fighting people that are my age. I'm supposed to kill them and they are supposed to kill us. What a waste of life.'"

Chapter Six

Iraq Celebrates its American Prisoners

After the interrogation came to an end, Hernandez and his peers were taken out of the building where a Red Cross ambulance awaited them. They were ordered to get in.

"The Iraqi soldiers tied our hands and feet with plastic ties," Hernandez stated. "They put a guard in the back with us with two Iraqis in front. Everyone had AK-47s and they told us that we were going to the hospital and drove away."

Without blindfolds on, Hernandez was able to look around and as he did, the American soldier noticed that the 30-something-year-old guard seated amongst them was staring at them with a "mean expression on his face."

"How did I get into this mess?" Hernandez silently thought to himself.

As they made their way down the road, Hernandez said he noticed a U.S. Army truck passing by and inside were roughly four or five Iraqi soldiers cheering as they grasped on tightly to their AK-47s.

"They were all jammed inside the truck, celebrating our capture just like the people on the streets," Hernandez recalled.

Driving alongside them were civilians, Fedayeen, and Iraqi soldiers all shooting their AK-47s in the air. Looking at one of the U.S. vehicles, Hernandez remembered seeing "507th" on the bumper.

"I also saw another truck I.D.," the American solider remembered. "I think it was 33 and I thought that truck belonged to one of my best friends, Specialist Jun Zhang. All I kept thinking was that those guys are probably dead because now the Iraqi soldiers are driving their trucks."

This was the first time reality sunk in. Hernandez realized that many of his friends were dead already. The Iraqis were celebrating the death of American soldiers; young men and women with families who would forever mourn their loss.

"I remember thinking about my friends...Zhang and Estrella and the other guys and I got really sad," Hernandez noted. "I said, 'Oh my God, these are my friends and they are probably dead and we are the only ones still alive.'

"We began quietly talking under our breath, trying to figure out who was driving which truck until the Iraqi soldiers told us, 'Shut up.' So, we just silently stared at each other, not knowing for sure that a bunch of our friends had been killed."

Arriving at a huge hospital, the ambulance pulled into the emergency area and through the windows, the POWs could see the drivers get out and talk to nurses and doctors who were emphatically shaking their heads, no. Irritated, the drivers got back into the ambulance and told the Americans that the hospital was full. They sped off as Hernandez wondered if they would live or if this was their last few minutes remaining until they reached the end of their collective road.

In the front passenger seat sat the doctor that had first aided them. He spoke better English than the rest of the captors and offered them a small sense of security. As the backseat guard kept staring the American soldiers down, and people on the streets continued cheering as they drove by, the doctor assured them, "You guys are going to be OK."

Later, Hernandez learned that the doctor was captured

and during his interrogation, he reported that the POWs were supposed to be executed once they arrived at their first location. However, rather than keep them there until Special Republican guards executed them, the doctor passed them off, letting the American soldiers leave to another destination.

"Someone actually gave me the doctor's email but I have never contacted him," stated Hernandez. "That was in 2005 and at the time I wanted to put Iraq behind me. I wasn't ready but someday, I will email him and thank him for saving us because he did save our lives."

At this point, Hernandez said that he viewed the Iraqis as "cold-blooded murderers" because "you could see the hatred in their eyes." Everywhere they drove, the Iraqi soldiers could be seen in their fighting positions, pointing machine guns at them behind sandbag barricades.

"Some of the soldiers," explained Hernandez, "were wearing jeans and a T-shirt with red and white checkered cloths wrapped around their heads.

"Soldiers were everywhere," he added. "I wondered, 'Could they possibly have more soldiers than us?'"

Arriving at an "old-style house," the ambulance stopped and the POWs were ordered to get out. As they piled out of the vehicle, Hernandez stood in front of the house that transformed into a prison once he walked inside. Later, Hernandez discovered this was one of many Saddam Hussein secret prisons scattered throughout Iraq.

Putting the group into one room, Hernandez asked to use the restroom. He was escorted to a run-down little area with a small sink and a hole in the ground, which was the toilet. Moments later, Hernandez returned to his peers where he saw a big bowl of what appeared to be chicken mixed with rice, tomato, and onion placed before the group. With their fingers, the Americans ate as the Iraqis did.

"What the hell is this?" wondered Hernandez.

For the first time, they were left completely alone, providing Miller with the opportunity to explain to Hernandez that Sloan, a member of their platoon, had died.

"He got shot in the head," said Miller.

"I was in shock," explained Hernandez. "It was so depressing. Sloan was only 19-years-old."

Just then, gunfire was overheard and the group simultaneously froze. A door opened and an Iraqi soldier walked in.

"Let's go!" he yelled.

Rushed back into the Red Cross ambulance, the driver sped off to another destination. Transported into a Japanese SUV, Hernandez, Riley, Hudson, and Miller were seated in the back and Johnson was placed up in front between two guards.

"I'm passing you off now," said the doctor. "You are now on your own. They are going to take you away. My job is done."

With the physician now gone, Hernandez grew fearful. He was their "safe guy." Hope, once again, grew very bleak.

As they left, one of the guards, seated next to Johnson and wearing civilian clothing, angrily began yelling at them in English.

"Why are you here?" he shrieked. "You are here for our oil!"

"I felt really bad," recalled Hernandez. "He said both Bush and [UK Prime Minister Tony Blair] Blair were criminals, trying to steal their oil.

"We were the enemy in their eyes and I thought to myself, 'This guy doesn't know why we are here. We were told that we are here to free the people and he doesn't know that."

Civilians gathered as the Iraqis driving them shouted, "Americans! Americans!" As they entered a small town, everyone grew excited over the "enemy's" arrival. Parking in front of the plaza area of a hotel, the Iraqi soldiers got out of their vehicle and continued yelling.

"Americans!" they screamed.

People swarmed the SUV and Hernandez said there must

have been 40 or more of them, singing and dancing.

"I thought of the movie *Black Hawk Down* and got scared," described Hernandez. "It felt so much like it. The buildings, the people, and the situation we were in. I remembered that one part of the movie when they surrounded the American soldier and tore him apart. When I watch it now, I get chills."

Women and children started banging on the windows as Hernandez became increasingly scared. And then they started throwing rocks.

"It was around 3PM and very, very hot," Hernandez explained. "The people were getting more and more excited. I remember a little girl about 7-years-old looking at us through the window. She looked innocent. So did the other kids."

As the adults grew more crazed, Hernandez recalled his entire group saying the same thing: "We are going to get killed."

"We might get lynched," added one of the American soldiers.

However, when the Iraqi soldiers got back into the SUV, the crowd backed off, and they drove to another town where the same nightmare was repeated. It became apparent to Hernandez that this may not be where they get mauled to death. Rather than a soon-to-be fatality, they were mere "trophies."

"We were no longer as scared because we realized they were just showing us off," Hernandez opined.

Two long hours later, the POWs were drenched in sweat due to the intense heat and non-existent air conditioning. As the sun beat down on Hernandez's face through the open window, he noticed that they arrived at an "old, poor city."

The American soldiers began whispering to each other, "We are in Baghdad." Climbing hills, the neighborhoods went from bad to better until they entered a "nice neighborhood" where Hernandez noted the wealthy people lived.

Fedayeens and Iraqi soldiers stood guard, holding their AK-47s as the prisoners pulled up to a very large home with a patio.

"A bunch of reporters were there with about ten camera-people," stated Hernandez. "They made us sit in a single file line. A Navy airplane, maybe a Hornet, flew right near us, very low. We got really scared and everyone around us scattered like rats."

After the plane left, the silence was a cue for the Iraqis to return. The Americans were then escorted into the house where they were seated in a room. Surrounded by Iraqi soldiers, their hands were untied and Riley and Miller asked for a cigarette.

"It was weird because they were being very nice to us," remembered Hernandez. "They even brought us some wine to drink. I was the only one who turned them down."

"You don't drink?" asked a young guy who spoke perfect English.

"It's against my religion," Hernandez replied.

When they offered cigarettes to everyone, Hernandez turned that down, too. The Iraqis laughed out loud. While most of the Iraqi soldiers had dark features, the men with blonde hair, pale skin and hazel-blue eyes surprised Hernandez. These Iraqis were part of the elite Special Republican Guard.

"You don't drink or smoke so what do you do?" asked another soldier as the rest of them chuckled.

Hernandez looked at the Special Republican Guard who was there to defend Baghdad as well as execute them, he discovered later, and forced a smile.

"One of the blonde soldiers gave me a look like, 'Why are you looking at me?' and I just turned away," Hernandez stated. "The leaders, though, kept telling us that we were going to be all right."

Whether that was true or not, he had no idea.

Chapter Seven

Scared to Death

Abruptly pushing through the front door, two imposing Iraqis in camouflage uniforms burst in and with thick, husky voices, they yelled at everyone, yanking the cigarettes and wine away from their prisoners. Looking like elementary school children who just got busted by the principle for skipping school, some of the Iraqi soldiers raced out of the room. One of the camouflaged men forcefully shoved the Americans' heads down low and Hernandez became frightened. Treating them as if they were hard-core criminals with no souls, the Iraqis grabbed their hands and slapped handcuffs back on them.

After strapping the American soldiers' feet together, they covered their heads with brown sacks.

"This was it," thought Hernandez. "I'm going to die."

They pulled the prisoners-of-war by the arms, forcing them outside and placing them in a circle. Hernandez said he lowered his head in his hands and began to cry.

"They are going to kill us," Hernandez continued to repeat to himself. "They are going to kill us for sure."

With his head fully covered, unable to see what was happening, Hernandez suddenly heard a familiar voice.

"Don't worry, you are going to be OK," stated the Iraqi soldier who kindly passed out wine to them earlier.

"At that moment," Hernandez said, "I began to calm down a bit, and I was trying really hard to stop crying."

"Stand up!" shouted another Iraqi soldier.

The roaring sound of trucks was overheard by the fearful American soldiers. After Hernandez's shoes were yanked off of his feet, he was pulled off the ground.

"I could feel that they had separated us and I was by myself," Hernandez mused. "I thought, 'Oh, my God, I'm alone now.'"

Hernandez was transplanted in a truck and they drove away. For hours, he sat with a bag over his head. "It was getting really cold and all this time," explained Hernandez, "one of the Iraqi soldiers had his knee in my ribs with his rifle pushing against my body.

"They were talking to each other and I guess they must have read my socks. I was wearing white Haines socks instead of our traditional black socks, and they kept repeating the words, 'Haines.'

"When we stopped, I could sense that it was nighttime. They took me inside a building and led me into a room where I was ordered to sit in a chair."

Once the sack was removed from his head, the American prisoner noticed a few mini-cameras and a reporter wearing jeans and a black shirt. With him was an officer in his mid-fifties wearing a "gray dress uniform." Reading off a piece of paper, the officer was asking the same questions.

"Where is the 82nd Airborne?" he asked. "Where are the Special Forces?"

"I don't know," Hernandez replied.

"Realizing that they weren't going to get any answers," said Hernandez, "they blindfolded me and took me out of the room. It felt like I was in a house and there was lots of commotion in the background. Luckily, when I was put into a dark room, my friends were there. We were all together again.

"I was feeling very tired from not having slept in several days and all I wanted to do was sleep. They pushed me down, and it was very uncomfortable because we were sitting on hard concrete."

Hernandez's eyes kept drooping and the urge to fall asleep was overwhelming. As his tired body began to slump to one side, a guard would violently kick him in the head.

"Get up!" bellowed the guard. "Get up!"

It was nearly impossible to sit upright, and each time his tired body began to slide down the wall, he was viciously hit in the head, back, and neck.

"I can't stay here like this," Hernandez thought. "If this is where they are going to keep us, I can't handle this."

Feeling desperate while he was sitting upright, suddenly he felt something warm hit him and drip down his body.

"They were pissing on us," he said. "It started smelling bad and I became angry. We were being disrespected. They laughed but there was nothing that we could do."

Soaked in the Iraqis' urine, Hernandez and his peers were ordered to stand up and once again, they were piled into a vehicle, leaving their current location and heading towards a new destination.

Arriving at a tall prison, the Americans were escorted

down a long hallway and placed in individual cells. Their handcuffs and blindfolds were removed. Hernandez recalled spotting a small window high up on the walls, which were covered with Arabic writing. Despite the cockroaches crawling all over the room, exhaustion got the better of him. Hernandez crept into a corner and slept for a few minutes.

Awakened abruptly by a few Iraqi soldiers who opened the door holding lamps, they tossed "some yellow outfits" into the cell, which had the black letters POW on them.

After putting on the yellow garb, a guard came by a few minutes later and signaled for Hernandez to change into another uniform that was similar but with stripes.

"They looked like pajamas," described Hernandez. "I was ordered to put on a pair of sandals, too."

Finally, he was given a little mat and pillow. After lying down, within seconds, this spiritually, mentally and physically drained American soldier closed his eyes and fell asleep for the night.

Chapter Eight

Day Two

As the sunlight shined through the barred windows, Hernandez opened his eyes to his second day as a prisoner-of-war.

"Men in civilian clothes with black and red colored cloths around their necks came to bring us breakfast," remembered Hernandez. "I was hungry and seeing the chicken with soup and tea was appetizing. But then I noticed my bullet wound. It had been bleeding all night because I slept on my side. I was tired before and didn't feel anything but now, I started feeling the pain."

In order to alleviate his suffering, Iraqi doctors changed Hernandez's bandage and gave him a shot.

"The needle was big," recalled Hernandez, "and I found out later that the other soldiers getting shots asked questions, wanting to know what they were giving us."

However, Hernandez was simply told that he was receiving two shots – one for pain and the other for infection. As the Americans sat in their separate cells, they tried communicating, speaking very loud, but were quickly shushed by enemy soldiers.

Chapter Nine

Surgery

Sitting in his cold cell on March 25, 2003, Hernandez said he could overhear strangers talking to one another.

Hearing other voices meant that there were at least two more people imprisoned with the American soldiers.

Chief Warrant Officer David Williams, age 31, and Chief Warrant Officer Ronald D. Young, age 26, of the 1-227 Helicopter Attack Battalion were the latest Iraqi captives.

"Who is there?" asked Williams.

"We are Americans," Hernandez and his co-captives stated.

"Shut up!" yelled an Iraqi soldier.

For a few long moments, everyone grew silent. Then, they began whispering to each other. The continuous communication kept Hernandez mentally strong; despite the Iraqis' stories of America's defeat.

"They kept playing mind games with us, saying that we were losing the war and losing many of our soldiers," Hernandez explained. "They also said that the American people didn't like us anymore."

Every few days, a doctor would come and let Hernandez out of his cell in order to give him shots in his butt. One day when he was scheduled for an X-ray, the building's front door was left ajar, and Hernandez caught a peek outside.

"There was a sandstorm," he stated. "Everything looked brownish-orange. I thought we were underground up until that moment."

As a result of the storm, all American missions had been cancelled. Ordered to write a card to the Red Cross, Hernandez broke down and started crying.

"Why are you crying?" asked a doctor.

"I want to go home," Hernandez replied.

He lifted up Hernandez's head and looked him in the eyes.

"Stop crying," he said. "Your family loves you and one day you are going to go home."

With a bit of hope restored, Hernandez wiped the tears from his eyes and slowly walked back to his cell. There were other visitors including an officer "with many stars" who came in specifically to see Hernandez.

"Where are you from?" asked the officer, surrounded by guards.

Hernandez described the officer as someone with a slight sense of humor who was attempting to make his prisoner laugh.

"Are you Christian?" the officer inquired.

"Yes," Hernandez answered.

"You are going to become Muslim," said the officer. "Do you like Muslim girls?"

The officer continued, "You are going to marry a beautiful Muslim girl."

Thinking his questions were bizarre, Hernandez thought to himself: "Am I going to get stuck in this place forever?"

Without any idea as to what was going to happen to him, Hernandez accepted his uncertain fate and tried to be grateful for each second he was still alive.

"During one of these doctor visits, he made me sign a paper that said I was going to get surgery," Hernandez stated. "I did have some faith in this doctor but it was still scary.

"All three of us – Johnson, Hudson and I were taken to a hospital, blindfolded with handcuffs and shackles on. I could sort of see the tile floors. It was very cold and when I sat down next to a guard on a couch, each time I tried to look up, they pushed my head back down."

Once Hernandez was called into a room where the surgery would take place, he fearfully walked with the guards and sat on a long table. Pulling out a camera, Hernandez tried to block his face from being photographed.

"Say cheese," ordered a doctor.

Unable to take his headshot, Hernandez was informed he was "going under."

"That's all I remember," the soldier noted. "I was back in my cell when I woke up."

"They came in a little while later and gave me a shot in the butt," Hernandez added. "They said it was pain medication and it did actually help."

As he sat in his cell, Hernandez recalled looking at the writing on the walls. He thought about a book he read in high school called *She Went To War: The Rhonda Corum Story*, about a female major held captive in Iraq for eight days in 1991. He silently wondered if maybe she had been at the same prison he was in now.

With all the intensity surrounding his recent capture, Hernandez sat in his dark jail cell for five days.

"I remember hearing a vehicle drive by every evening," Hernandez recalled. "They would pray over loud speakers and it would go on for hours."

Being so far from home and hearing their prayers made things worse.

"I felt so weak and I could not do anything but think of home and my fellow soldiers who died in combat."

Chapter Ten

Thinking of Home

Born in McAllen, Texas on May 27, 1981, Edgar Hernandez was raised in Reynosa, Mexico but due to his United States citizenship, Hernandez's mom wanted him to attend school in the U.S. Along with his younger sister and two brothers, they moved into a small room at his grandparents' house in Alton, Texas and began attending an elementary school in Rio Grande Valley, which is a border town on the Gulf of Mexico.

The population in Rio Grande Valley was mostly

Hispanic, however, the majority of people spoke Spanish and English. Hernandez believed he fell short, academically.

"It was hard for me because a lot of the kids who knew English assumed I did, too," Hernandez said. "I would get embarrassed because when they tried to talk to me in English, I had to tell them that I didn't know the language. A lot of them didn't want to associate with me because of that."

With his father remaining behind in Reynosa to sell brooms and mops while trying to keep the money flow coming in, young Edgar struggled with the change. Although he lived in a tiny room that allowed zero privacy, this soldier-in-the-making felt lonely.

"I was really quiet and my teachers kept encouraging me to practice my English," remembered Hernandez. "I was just so shy and while my friends spoke both English and Spanish, I did pick up on some of the words but I was still very bad at it.

"It wasn't until I decided to join the Army that I really had to speak English. Even during all my high school years, I spoke Spanish with my friends."

Enlisting in the Army was not an impulsive decision for Hernandez. Since a very young age, he was highly interested in the military. Hernandez clearly remembered watching the news in Mexico and seeing the latest updates on Desert Storm. Something about that particular war captured Hernandez's attention at 10-years-old.

"After seeing Desert Storm on television," explained Hernandez, "my brothers and I would play war."

Even before Hernandez relocated to the United States permanently, he recalled telling his mother about his dream of joining the United States Army.

"No, you are not!" retorted his mother. "When you go to the U.S., you are going to go to college and get an education. You are not joining the military."

Regardless of his mother's reluctance, Hernandez held onto his dream. He took criminal justice classes during his junior and senior year of high school. Living in a difficult situation with little money and grandparents who were very strict and unenthused about all of their house guests, Hernandez passed the time by plotting his future. When Hernandez was 13, his father left Mexico and joined the family in the United States; however, the Hernandez clan still couldn't afford to live on their own.

After graduating from high school, Hernandez took the initiation test to enroll into the Army and failed. However, this didn't deter the hopeful soldier from pushing forward. He may have gotten hit in round one but there were many more rounds to go, and nothing was going to knock this determined young man out for good.

"I was told to wait six months and than re-take the exam," Hernandez noted. "So, I went to South Texas Community College for one semester. I would go to the library every chance I got and study for the ASVAV test. After the second try, I passed."

Along with his mother's pleads not to join, Hernandez's grandparents were also discouraging him. However, his father never stood in his way.

"It's your life," his dad encouraged. "You can do whatever you want."

Edgar left for boot camp in January 2000. Although he wanted to go for infantry airborne, his family and Pentecostal church, which he belonged to at the time, convinced the soldier not to do it.

"I wanted to be hard-core," remembered Hernandez, "but I had all these people telling me not to join because it was too dangerous. My mom said I was going to go to war and get killed, and the people in my church said I would go to hell because I might kill another human being."

After eight weeks of boot camp in Fort Jackson, South Carolina where he was introduced to other ethnicities for the first time, followed by AIT School in Fort Lee, Virginia, Hernandez was assigned as a supply clerk in El Paso, Texas. Already growing tremendously from his experience, Hernandez said that up until he joined the Army, mainly Hispanic people surrounded him. Now, he had stepped into a world where all colors mixed. It was definitely a culture shock but a great learning experience.

Hernandez described his boot camp experience as being relatively easy. Rather than feeling frightened or overwhelmed, he was excited. With pride, he learned how to shoot an M-16 and clean a weapon. He also threw a live grenade for the first time. Hernandez joined the Army for the experience as well as the opportunities it offered. After returning from war, he gained an entirely new perspective on things.

"I now realize that I did this for my country," Hernandez declared. "This country gave my parents a chance at a better life. We were given food stamps to live on and because of that we were able to survive.

"I have a lot of things in my life that I would never have had if we stayed in Mexico. I am proud to serve the United States military. It is worth it to me."

Chapter Eleven

Life After 9-11

Life on the Army base had been a welcome reprieve of routine and stability for young Edgar Hernandez. That is until the morning of Tuesday, September 11, 2001, when 19 Al Qaeda affiliated terrorists boarded four commercial passenger jet airliners, which resulted in roughly 3,000 deaths—the World Trade Center collapsing, the Pentagon destruction and United Airlines Flight 93 crashing into a field.

"When September 11th came it was like a shock," recalled

Hernandez.

Having just finished physical training, the solider clearly recalls watching the news and seeing a fire in one of the towers of the World Trade Center in New York City.

"They mentioned an airplane had hit the right tower," Hernandez vividly recounted. "And I saw the other plane hit the second tower. I freaked out. I remember the reporter was scared. She couldn't find the words. She had to continue talking but you could tell she was in shock.

"We started hearing about the Pentagon and of the other airplanes. Everybody just panicked. They locked down the base and nobody could go in or out."

Confusion and tension soon filled the base and by the following day, talk of retaliation and war had been ignited.

"I was scared," Hernandez confessed. "I signed up just so I could do my time and get out. I didn't want to go to war."

Two months later, the United States attacked Afghanistan for harboring members of the terrorist organization, Al Qaeda.

Life on the base became tension-filled as soldiers dealt with one recall after another. These recalls consisted of packing your own duffle bag and gear and heading to the Army airbase to ship out overseas.

"People were worried," Hernandez noted, "especially the new people. The older soldiers told us not to worry, though, because we are going to be behind enemy lines. Our jobs are to shoot missiles from far away. So, it's going to be safe."

Hernandez said that he wasn't surprised when President George W. Bush began publicly talking about Iraq and their ownership of biological weapons and full support of Al Qaeda. As a result, Hernandez and his unit were trained in case of a nuclear, biological or chemical attack.

"The commander told us, 'We are going to train to go to war with Iraq.' This was a few months after September 11."

While the world and the media focused on the ongoing war in Afghanistan, the military was already planning to go to war in Iraq.

"This was October 2001 and everyone on the base was making a big deal about Iraq," Hernandez explained. "We were training and gearing up for our combat mission. The war had begun and it was just a matter of time before we were off."

Chapter Twelve

Proud American Soldiers Off to War

Stationed in El Paso, Texas, Hernandez bonded with a small crew who became his support group during this tumultuous time.

"I met my Squad Leader, Specialist Aldo Magana, a Hispanic from Brownsville, Texas," said Hernandez. "That was cool. I remember he came to me and spoke in Spanish. He made me feel less homesick.

Along with Magana, Hernandez's click from the Bravo

Battery unit included Specialist Fernando Guerra and Specialist Aaron Hernandez.

"The four of us would always hang out together," stated Hernandez.

By spring of 2002, the 507th Maintenance Company was short on soldiers and was picking candidates from the Air Batteries, thus, taking Hernandez. "Here I was thinking about a vacation in Hawaii and now I was being transferred. I was lucky and met my best friend Estrella when I arrived to my new unit."

As the possibility of deployment to Iraq became more realistic, Hernandez stated that he was ready and willing to go. The thought of dying didn't cross his mind.

"The politicians were still debating," Hernandez said, "and although we believed we were probably going to end up going to Iraq, I did not feel as if we were in danger. I didn't suspect we'd be actually going to war."

Even before American civilians knew they were gearing up for a face-off with Iraq, the soldiers were told that Iraq was violating the "No Fly Zone" as well as "shooting scud missiles." Hernandez remembered watching the news during the months of December through February 2003, and finally the ambitious young soldier got word that on February 15, 2003, he would be going to the Middle East.

"I spent Valentine's Day with my girlfriend, said goodbye to my family and the following day," recalled Hernandez, "I drove my car to Estrella's house.

"His mom [Amalia Estrella-Soto] and the rest of the family were crying. I told her that we were going to be fine. Our job was safe because we'd be working at a distance, shooting missiles at far-away targets, as a support unit."

With a 2PM roll call, the two friends jumped into Estrella's car and headed off. The young soldiers arrived on base and saw everyone gathering at a formation area with all of their families. Hernandez, however, asked his girlfriend and family not to come.

"It would be too painful," he said.

Around 10PM, families sobbed as they watched their loved ones pile into long, white buses, taking the soldiers to the gym on base. When they arrived, Hernandez and the other soldiers walked into a building, checked all of their bags and waited for a few hours.

"I was sitting there with Estrella," Hernandez recalled, "and we started feeling sad as we looked at the night lights.

"This is it," he added. "We are off to the Middle East."

Before they boarded an aircraft at Biggs Army Airfield, the soldiers were given gifts such as CD's along with other personal possessions.

As he and his peers walked onto the plane, a flight attendant standing at the front door greeted them with a sympathetic smile.

"Good luck," she said.

As the soldier thought about her "well wishes," it struck him as odd. Up until now, he never considered this to possibly be the beginning of the end. Reality started to finally set in. Leaving El Paso, the soldiers were flown to New Jersey, then Frankfurt, Germany before finally reaching their destination, Kuwait.

Chapter Thirteen

My Best Friend Estrella

Amidst the chaos and frustration of going to war and having become a POW, Edgar Hernandez was, and still is, deeply saddened by the loss of his best friend.

In April of 2002, Hernandez, stationed at a military base in Texas, was transferred to the very strict 507th (which is now extinct due to the tragic occurrences that happened to the POWs.)Working long hours, 6AM to 10AM everyday, including some weekends became the norm. Supporting an entire battalion—nearly five batteries—was exhausting.

By October of 2002, units from the base began deploying to Kuwait. Having grown up watching Desert Storm on TV, Hernandez, now age 21, was readying himself for his own real-life, overseas war experience.

A member of the 507th, Hernandez quickly bonded with Estrella. "We worked so hard and hated it," recalled Hernandez. "We were loading all the vehicles and gear and sent them off to Kuwait."

Days before heading out to Iraq, Hernandez, Zhang, Duboi, Estrella and his girlfriend, and Sloan were in 21-year-old Private First Class Howard Johnson's room. "We told jokes and talked about being away from home. We didn't know when we would be returning from Iraq."

Chapter Fourteen

Kuwait City

When the American soldiers arrived in Kuwait, they were taken to a large military base, which was their reception camp. With multiple tents aligned, Hernandez entered one of them where a general waited for his new troops.

Briefed on the culture in this Middle Eastern country, Hernandez said he was told not to associate with the women.

"We were told that the women must walk behind their

husbands," remembered Hernandez. "They are not allowed to drive. Basically, women were not considered equal to men and we were ordered not to even look at them."

It was very hot during the day and the loose sand stuck to the soldiers' sweaty skin. At night, however, the temperature drastically dropped. According to Hernandez, "It went from 130 degrees to 90 degrees."

Although 90 degrees still seems hot because the temperature is so high during the day, it feels as if the weather gets very cold at night and soldiers were often wearing heavy jackets to keep warm.

Shortly after their arrival to the first reception camp, which was a permanent base, the American soldiers were escorted onto a bus. Packed in, Hernandez said they drove for hours with soldiers crashing on the floors. Finally, they arrived at Camp Virginia, which was in the middle of nowhere.

"We entered the base covered with sand and were assigned our sleeping area in one of the tents," remembered the soldier.

For two weeks during February 2003, Hernandez was stationed at Camp Virginia with little to do.

"All the equipment travels by ship," Hernandez explained, "so we waited, played pool in the recreational tent, made phone calls back home and were even able to use a computer. I spent a lot of time with Estrella. We ate pizza and listened to music a lot."

The wait seemed like it was forever. There were no air conditioners and the weather became increasingly unbearable. Due to the sand blowing non-stop, if you do not completely dry off after a shower, it will stick to you.

"That is why the Middle Eastern men don't like to shower," quipped Hernandez.

Once their vehicles arrived, Hernandez was ordered to drive in a three-truck convoy to pick up supplies.

"Since I was a supply clerk," he explained, "I had to go on some dangerous missions that entailed getting some of the sergeants and taking them to another camp.

"All the squads had a machine gunner with them. I had a license to drive a five-ton truck and semi-trailers as well as Humvees. We would take turns driving.

"We drove back and forth from Camp Doha and also went to Camp New York, Camp Udairi and Camp New Jersey – all near the border of Iraq."

Driving to Camp Doha was a luxury. Being stuck in the middle of nowhere and feeling attacked by the sand as it clung to their skin causing the soldiers to uncomfortably itch all over, Hernandez cherished his time away from Camp Virginia. Going to the local Burger King at Camp Doha was a real treat in comparison to the mess hall, which Hernandez described as "terrible."

"Our daily routine would be to get up in the morning, run for two miles on the loose sand, shower, build secure barbed wire areas for all the parts, wait for more trucks and run missions.

February rolled into March and most of the soldiers "hated being there." They were homesick and bored.

"We would say, 'Man, if we are going to war,'" the solider recalled, 'let's get it over with.'"

Chapter Fifteen

Shock and Awe

Standing atop his Humvee manning a 50-caliber machine gun while on guard duty, Hernandez said, "It was weird because I noticed lots of planes taking off from the nearby airport towards Iraq. This went on for most of my guard duty."

The next morning, March 20, 2003, the soldiers were informed the war had begun. "We heard back home they called this mission Shock And Awe, and Operation Iraqi Freedom," Hernandez recalled. "We were in Kuwait for about a month when the ground war had begun. We were supposed to be six hours behind the combat units as we were part of the supply, and would be firing missiles from a distance. I was pretty excited and not too concerned with being killed."

With war underway, the soldiers began their formation and lined up all of the vehicles that would be used for their convoy. They were briefed about potential sniper fire and told to just keep driving no matter what.

As a means to inspire the troops, the soldiers were told before the cameras of CNN and the rest of the world, "We are going to free Iraq!"

"I got nervous and said this is something big," Hernandez explained. "Some people were saying, 'Let's go kick some butt.' We hoped it wouldn't last long."

Preparing to battle the fourth largest Army in the world, Hernandez noted he was a bit apprehensive. "They had many soldiers but we had more equipment. I was a little scared but I was pumped up. The colonel mentioned, 'This is a part of history.'"

"We got in our trucks and were in a huge convoy. We had 8,000 vehicles just from Camp Virginia, the 3rd Infantry Division, so there was a lot of sand being thrown up around us. We traveled throughout the night, resting in Kuwait until dawn. Our group, the 507th, was formed by 64 soldiers and traveled in countless vehicles. We were part of a supply chain and our cargo included spare parts for our weapons batteries, fuel and water tankers."

Crossing the border into Iraq, a nervous Hernandez saw numerous burned Russian-made tanks left from Desert Storm.

"It looked like a museum," he noted.

By the early evening, Hernandez admitted, "Things began to get a little confusing. We were driving three trucks side-by-side and some were breaking down and getting left behind. There were lots of traffic jams and as we drove down the road, some units were beginning to get mixed up. You could tell there was some confusion. We stopped several times to get gas but we drove all night, bumper-to-bumper in the middle of the desert.

"Late in the night, my truck started giving me trouble," Hernandez remembered. "My transmission was getting jammed and the gears got stuck. It would not move. I jumped out and Specialist James Kiehl, age 22, someone who was later killed in battle, helped me fix my vehicle."

Looking at a sea of red lights in front of him as the convoy continued into the night, Hernandez recalled, "It looked cool; we looked mean; bad ass."

Yet the "bad ass" convoy kept breaking down while making its way across the desert, climbing over sand dunes designed for tanks and not these giant supply vehicles.

The next morning, March 22, 2003, the commander came back on "Police Call," (a term in the military for pick up and move out), and gathered everyone who had a broken-down vehicle, including Hernandez. They numbered 18 trucks in all.

"We had our weapons and drove all day and started falling behind," Hernandez, who hadn't slept in days, recounted.

Right before sunset, another truck in the new convoy of 18 rundown vehicles, gave out.

"We felt we could not leave this vehicle behind so we had to wait until it was fixed."

Hernandez off to training before
being deployed to Iraq

Specialist Diaz, Chase and
Specialist Edgar Hernandez

Edgar with friends at AIT Training

507th Maintenance Command
group photo

G Company, 8th Platoon, Ruff Ryders, Fort Lee,
Virginia, group photo; Edgar in back row July, 2000

(Top) Pvt. Pace, Spc. Gonzalez, Spc. Hernandez
Spc. Batista (bottom) Pvt. Estrella, Sgt. Gonzalez
PFC Elliot and Specialist name unknown

Friend, Hernandez, Cruz and Garcia

Hernandez, Estrella and friend

Chapter Sixteen

Here Come the Bombs

With the bombs growing closer, their explosive sounds jolted Hernandez away from his thoughts of home and the first days of battle, returning him to an unsettling present.

As one bomb hit really close, it felt like the walls were cracking and dust was flying everywhere.

"We started screaming, 'Get us out of here,'" Hernandez recalled. "And I started praying with the blanket on top of me."

Left alone during the air raid, the POWs quickly started to plot their escape, knowing death was assured if they remained.

"We were alone for about one hour and were desperate to get out," Hernandez recounted. "Williams said, 'Let's try anything,' as the bombs kept coming. I could hear Johnson screaming."

When the bombs stopped, all the Iraqi soldiers came back laughing, which angered Williams. "They told us the bomb hit like 50 meters from us," Hernandez recalled, "and that we were safe and not to worry. But Williams told them that we were going to get bombed and they said, 'Don't worry, this place can take a bomb.' Williams kept telling them this place is going to get blown up but they just laughed."

A few minutes after the bombs stopped, the doors were opened, and the POWs were relieved to know they were being moved again. Handcuffed, with their feet tied and blind-folded the American soldiers were put back in the Red Cross ambulance.

"All seven of us were together now," Hernandez explained. "But, we still hadn't seen the pilots' faces. We only knew them by their voices. We drove for about 40 minutes."

Later, the POWs learned that their previous location had been bombed and destroyed. "We got lucky," Hernandez mused, thinking about what could have been.

At their next place of captivity, the U.S. soldiers again found themselves in one of Hussein's secret prisons, this time a light green, two-story house. Taken upstairs to their own individual cells, they were each given a bowl and spoon. The soldiers remained there for two full days.

Just as in their previous cells, there was Arabic writing on the walls. "I never saw American writing on the walls and I was always looking," Hernandez said. "I never wrote my name but I think the other soldiers did and one even drew an American flag."

From time-to-time, a doctor would come in and change their bandages. Reunited with the same guards from the previous prison, Hernandez recalled their captors had no interest in knowing their prisoners, except for one Iraqi solider who would ask Hernandez questions in secret.

"He would talk to me when he would take me to the WC (water closet) but I could barely understand him. I would ask him if we were going home and he would say, 'yes.' I kind of built a friendship with him and he told me that the American soldiers were surrounding Baghdad.

"Where are you from?" asked the friendly Iraqi solider.

"Texas," Hernandez answered.

"Oh, George Bush's home," the Iraqi solider replied.

"He also told me that he saw my mother on the news,"

Hernandez continued. "I felt bad about my mom being so worried but was relieved that she knew I was alive. He said he saw my two brothers on the news, too. He told me this is in secret while I was in the bathroom because the other guards always told us we were losing the war."

With at least one friend in Iraq, Hernandez was able to deal with the harsh reality that his other captors weren't as pleasant.

Two days into their stay at this location, everyone heard helicopters flying by. As the Iraqi soldiers opened fire on the choppers, the American captives yelled to the Iraqis not to shoot or they would get bombed.

But they kept firing at the helicopters, anyway. Then they came for the soldiers. Blindfolded, they took them away again.

"They were in a rush because they felt they were going to come back and drop a bomb," Hernandez explained. "So, all seven of us left in the Red Cross ambulance."

Afterwards, Hernandez learned that once again their location had been destroyed by U.S. forces.

Taking off, the ambulance soon was mired in Baghdad traffic. "I was blindfolded and could not see," Hernandez remembered. "I tried looking up. It was daytime and we drove for many minutes. It was very hot."

Brought to another one of Hussein's secret prisons; this one was a one-story house.

"At this prison I asked to use the bathroom and saw a picture of Saddam Hussein," Hernandez pointed out. "There was a guard sitting at the desk with the picture behind him. What I remember from this prison were the two pilots mentioning that the 4th Infantry Division should already be here. I could hear the pilots from my cell.

"At this prison, the guards must have been running out of food because one day all we ate were cucumbers. The water was in a plastic container and it looked grey and dirty. For two days, I did not drink it."

As the other captives became ill from a variety of circumstances, Hernandez would only ever wet his lips with the foul water. Without ventilation, the only air in the cramped room came from a small, bar-covered window. On the verge of passing out from dehydration, Hernandez struggled with keeping his grip on reality. The quiet neighborhood was filled with sounds of singing birds as the war roared on.

Chapter Seventeen

A New Face

Moved to a new prison, this time Hernandez found himself in the same cell as Hudson and an unfamiliar face.

"Who are you?" Hudson questioned.

"Chief Warrant Officer Young," answered the unknown prisoner.

Seeing Young for the very first time, he turned and climbed up to the window, pushing aside the cardboard blocking his view and peered out. He saw some bunkers and people outside, as well as wires running to the house. He believed they were going to blow up the building.

Caught looking out, the guards removed Young from the cell and brought in his co-pilot, Williams, whom the 507th POWs had never seen either. As Williams was escorted into the cell, he began to ask the Iraqi soldiers if they were going to kill them. And they retorted, "Allah is Great," which did not calm their fears.

Looking at Williams, Hernandez asked, "Sir, do you think I will be home in time for my birthday?" Breaking the tension with a much-needed moment of levity, Williams pointed out later, "We were hurting so bad, scared for our lives and in so much danger. That moment of laughter was a huge moral win for us."

Captive for approximately 12 days, this time the prisoners were visited by a doctor in a wrinkled and muddy "cheap attorney suit." He told the Americans in English that a bomb came very close to his car and it flipped over three times.

"What was funny," Hernandez recalled, "is that he looked like he was wearing a wig because his hair was moving around. He was laughing about his accident and we were laughing about his hair. He described the whole scene and Williams asked him if his car had seat belts and he said, no. It was a Japanese car and we laughed some more. Then, he tended to our injuries and gave us medicine as the guards brought us food."

By this time, Williams had become the unofficial leader of the group. Having undergone POW training for pilots, he explained to everyone that it was important to keep everybody's hopes up.

"I remember we were about to go to bed and you could hear a gun battle going on outside; explosions and lots of bullets."

Chapter Eighteen

100 MPH

All night long the captive soldiers heard gunfire and bombs going off outside. Finally, the soldier was able to get a little sleep. Hernandez awoke the next morning just as the sun was coming out. Roosters and dogs could be heard amidst the gun battle that was still going on—a crazy combination of life in Iraq.

But then it was time for the same routine to begin again. A doctor would come in and change the prisoners' bandages; then allowed them to eat. Soon after, another firefight could be heard as planes flew above outside.

Williams said it was an AT-10 War Dog because of the sound they made. He was teaching everyone how to identify planes by their sound. He said this plane had a machine gun in the front. That was why it sounded as if it were very close. As the Iraqi soldiers began shooting at the plane, it would sound off with thousands of rounds of bullets followed by silence.

"Basically, they were getting killed," Hernandez explained, "and we began to feel joy from them dying. It seemed funny because they would repeat the same thing again and again. The Iraqi soldiers would shoot at the planes flying by, and then they would get sprayed by thousands of bullets. We were laughing because they were not learning their lesson, which was not to shoot the airplane. It was so close, we could hear all the casing from the bullets falling on the roof."

Immediately, the group was taken to another location. This procedure of being rounded up; tied up and taken somewhere else was, as Hernandez noted, "getting old for us."

With their eyes blind-folded and hands in cuffs, the Red Cross ambulance housing the POWs was racing at nearly 100 miles-per-hour. "We were all scared because we could not see," Hernandez recounted. "We were passing cars and there were gun battles everywhere. Then, there was a huge explosion in front of us as a big fireball went off."

Afterwards, Marines explained to Hernandez that they

believed Iraqi officers were trying to escape in the Red Cross ambulance and they were attempting to blow it up.

Chapter Nineteen

Conversations in the Dark

After the helter-skelter ambulance ride from Hell, Hernandez found himself in a new prison, this one a cramped, pitch black cell. The only difference this time was that he was not alone. Sharing his confined quarters with Williams, the tired and weary soldier finally was able to speak to an ally.

"This was the first time I got to interact with someone, and that is something we no longer take for granted," Hernandez expressed. "To be confined and not have those basic needs, the ability to interact, it is very difficult; to go days without speaking to someone."

Holed up in an extremely uncomfortable squatting area, getting to know Williams helped keep Hernandez sane during this ordeal.

"We really got to know each other," the young soldier recounted. "He liked tattoos. Most of them honored the different units he had served. He told me of his plan to get a large POW tattoo on his back when he returned home."

The two burgeoning buddies even made promises of things they would do if they made it back home. "Williams promised he would take me flying one day," Hernandez said.

Unable to get any sleep in his tiny room, luckily, they were only confined at the prison for 24 hours.

"I will never forget those precious conversations, which inspired me and kept my hopes up," Hernandez stated.

Suddenly, without any notice, they were off again; the same jarring routine of being blindfolded and taken to a new location.

Chapter Twenty

Fuck Iraq!

Unlike the previous destinations, Hernandez and his fellow troops arrived at a house that didn't resemble a prison inside. The doors were barricaded but the guards were exceptionally "cool."

"The guards were, like, 15-years-old," Hernandez recalled. "And they didn't want to scare us."

"Are we winning the war?" asked an American soldier.

"Yes, and you guys are all famous in the United States," a guard replied.

Looking directly at Hernandez, he added, "I saw your mom and family on television. President Bush was talking about you, too."

"Did you see my family?" Williams asked.

"No. Your family don't love you," a guard retorted.

They all burst out laughing. For the first time, Hernandez noticed that the gigantic barrier separating the Americans and Iraqis felt as if it was getting chipped away.

"I realized that some of the guards here in Iraq were actually nice guys," Hernandez explained. "They were just doing their job."

Suddenly, a "tall guy" wearing a white gown and "70's style, CHiPS look-alike sunglasses," carrying an AK-47 waltzed into the room and the laughter abruptly simmered down. You could hear a pin drop on the floor as even the young Iraqi guards looked at this man with wide eyes, unsure as to what would happen next. He slowly took off his glasses and shouted, "FUCK IRAQ!"

Hernandez, shocked, looked at his fellow American soldiers. None of them were sure if this was really happening.

"What did he say?" questioned one of the Americans.

"FUCK IRAQ!" the man in white shouted again.

He then pulled out the keys to the Red Cross ambulance and tried to hand them to the American soldiers.

"Go, go!" said the young guard.

Although the other guards stopped him from handing over the keys, the Iraqis told Hernandez and his fellow prisoners that they would be going home soon. Then, the Iraqi guards left the room.

"I think they want us to leave," Williams declared. "They are scared and don't want us here. They are risking their own lives with us here."

According to Hernandez, Williams began making a "get-away plan." He said, "If they give us the keys to the ambulance and we take off, everyone is going to know we are Americans.

"Especially you, Miller," noted Williams. "You've got blonde hair and blue eyes."

Concluding that just driving off could be dangerous, Williams continued, "If we are going to get out of here, we may need to dress up like Iraqis."

Looking at Hernandez, he added, "You and Hudson should drive."

The group began making jokes about their "escape scenario." Williams ripped off his shirt and wrapped it around his head, pretending to be an Iraqi. Despite their capture, each soldier held onto his or her spirit, and laughter amongst tragedy proved to be the perfect remedy for survival.

"At this location," remembered Hernandez, "we had the best time."

Three days later, however, the American soldiers were moved once again. In handcuffs, shackles, and with their eyes covered, the POWs next location awaited them.

Chapter Twenty-One

Everybody Loves Raymond

"When we arrived at our location," Hernandez pointed out, "they took our blindfolds off. We were standing in front of a really big, beautiful home where a whole new set of guards resided."

Wearing uniforms with white stars, these new captors were policemen. The POWs could tell because a gold star represented the military. The vibe coming from the guards was positive. It became apparent that Hernandez and his crew were in a relatively safe place.

"Could you please bring us new bandages?" asked Williams.

Along with new bandages to wrap their wounds, one of the guards' wives cooked them a "great meal," which the American soldiers devoured. They also were given playing cards and dominoes. Thus, the Iraqis and Americans enjoyed each other's company over a good game of cards, food and conversation.

"We laughed at how smelly we all were," remembered Hernandez. "Weeks without showers or toilet paper—we smelled really, really bad."

Telling stories about their country, the Iraqis educated the Americans on their culture.

"They told us about the Sunni and Shia Iraqi people," Hernandez stated.

"I am Sunni," said one of the 30-something-year-old guards. "Our country has been at war for 20 years with Iran."

The guard became very emotional and as tears fell from his eyes, he continued, "The Iraqi Army is forcing us to watch you. We are so tired of being at war. I hope one day, we are free like the United States. I hope for a better Iraq."

The room was completely silent as this Iraqi man continued to cry. Hernandez felt like crying, as well. He thought about how difficult it must have been to constantly be trapped in a never-ending war.

"Listen, we will take care of you," added the guard. "Please don't try to escape. We don't want to make a mistake and piss off the Army. We are scared for our lives and the lives of our families."

For three full days, Hernandez said that he and his friends were treated very well. The Iraqis passed out cigarettes, as well as Cokes and Pepsi. "One of the guards," stated Hernandez, "looked like Raymond from the television show *Everybody Loves Raymond*.

"We aren't allowed to show our feet because it is seen as an insult," stated a guard while shuffling playing cards.

Suddenly, "Raymond" walked into the room with more sodas and everyone turned to look at him.

"Raymond!" they shouted.

Smiling, "Raymond" acknowledged them with a nod and took a seat. The cards were dealt and the game continued.

Chapter Twenty-Two

Planning the Rescue

Removed from his slumber, Williams was taken in the middle of the night from the rest of the group. Waiting for his return, after hours had passed, Hernandez and the others finally fell asleep. The next morning, to their surprise, Williams was with them.

"Hey, what happened?" asked Hernandez.

"The Marines are close by," Williams whispered leaning in. "Raymond" and the other Iraqis are plotting to help us get home safely. The Chief of Police's wife is going to give a note to the Marines, along with a map to this house so they can come and rescue us."

The American soldiers glanced at one another in disbelief. It seemed so surreal that this whole ordeal might soon be over and they would actually get out of it alive.

Chapter Twenty-Three

The Rescue

The Iraqis looked the American soldiers in their eyes and told them firmly not to tell anyone that they were instrumental in their escape.

"Tell them you were rescued," said an Iraqi soldier. "Otherwise, we will be killed. Our families will be killed."

Sworn to secrecy, the American and Iraqi soldiers were teaming up, and the Iraqis were going against their own Army to save American lives.

"One morning, we were eating breakfast and playing cards, Hernandez explained. "A guard walks in and told us that the Marines are now very close. He said, 'It's time. You guys are going home.'"

The American soldiers sat there in disbelief. Momentarily, they began hearing "a metal sound against the pavement." The tanks were coming.

"I tried to look outside the window," Hernandez stated.

Raising his voice, Williams abruptly said, "Dude, the battalion is passing us by. They are passing us!"

Panicked, he jumped up, ran to the window and started screaming.

"We are here!" shouted Williams. "We are here! We are Americans!"

"David, don't do that!" yelled a concerned Iraqi captain. "Don't scream!"

"They are going to pass us," shrieked Williams to the guards.

He then ripped off his brown shirt and wrote USA on it. Asking for permission to hang it outside the window, the Captain obliged. Staring at Williams, Hernandez watched as he began screaming and crying.

"They see us now," Williams yelled. "They are here!"

Johnson began to sob as Hernandez peeked out the window. He watched the Marines pull security around the house, keeping passersby away. Even one of the police officers that pulled in was told to get away but he didn't listen. With their rifles pointing at him, the Iraqi officer stepped out of his vehicle and got down on the ground. His weapon was apprehended.

BANG, BANG, BANG, the soldiers heard at the front door.

Several Marines broke down the door and rushed the room. All of the Iraqis got down on the ground and were stripped of their weapons. An Iraqi translator from California who accompanied the Marines began to speak.

"All the Americans get up!" he ordered.

Slowly, the soldiers began to pick themselves up off the floor.

"Move in a single file line," the interpreter continued.

Without shaving for three weeks, the Americans had beards and appeared dark-skinned from the lack of bathing. One of the Marines looked directly at Hudson, asking if he was American.

"Hell yeah, I am an American!" Hudson yelled.

"Move out, move out!" they continued. Enthusiastic, the Americans smiled from ear-to-ear as they left the house for good.

Being the first one out the door, Hernandez stepped onto an outside patio and noticed that Marines were everywhere—on the roof, along the side of the house, and positioned inside their AF Track vehicles with machine guns.

Escorted safely to the Marine trucks, suddenly, the just freed American soldiers grew worried about their Iraqi friends. Watching the Marines act bullish to the Iraqi police officers, Williams jumped out of the vehicle and ran back towards the house.

"Don't hurt these guys," he said. "They are good people."

Hernandez watched as Williams "got into it" with a Marine Major. "I am a Chief Warrant Officer and these guys are good people," stated Williams. "You better not hurt them."

"Get back in line!" barked the Major.

Williams returned to the AF Tracks and they drove off, this time in American operated vehicles. Although the soldiers were no longer afraid of their next destination, Hernandez recalled wondering if they would make it there safely. They hadn't been released from their fears just yet.

It was roughly 11AM and the soldiers were dead silent, hoping that their rescue would not end in a tragic firefight. They drove a few blocks and the Major looked at them.

"I'm so happy you are OK," he said. "A lady had come to us with a map. At first, we couldn't find the house. We thought it was an ambush, some sort of trap. Still, we followed up, thank God."

Hernandez and the former captives began sobbing, grateful to have survived. Arriving at a school, which was the Marines "safe house," the soldiers were given food made by one of the Iraqi people. As they devoured their meal and sipped it down with sodas, the interpreter approached them and shook their hands.

"We offered the Iraqi officers back at the house money and safety but they refused," the interpreter explained. "We offered to take them to the United States and they refused that, too. They said they loved their country and so we had no choice but to just let them go."

As the Marines called in a helicopter to come and pick up the American heroes, they were told to change into different clothing. Wearing soccer jerseys, the soldiers were then escorted to the Chinook helicopter.

"Thanks and good luck," Hernandez said to the Marines.

Suddenly, Hernandez realized that he gave the Marines the same well-wishes a flight attendant offered him right before he boarded a plane, heading to war. Although then, he didn't understand how precious his life would become, as a result of his capture, he now understood. Regardless of age, strength, gender, ethnicity, faith, and will-to-survive, stepping into a war zone means that there is only a 50/50 chance you will return safely.

The American heroes were lifted off the ground and Hernandez said he watched as they flew right above rooftops. Suddenly, he began hearing gunfire and felt his stomach turn.

"Oh, my God," he said. "They are going to shoot us down."

Chapter Twenty-Four

Meet the Press

Free at last, the ex-POWs were safe and on April 13, 2003, the soldiers were flown by helicopter, south of Iraq to an old airport. All the major news outlets were present, waiting for their arrival. As the soldiers emerged, they were swarmed by the likes of CBS, ABC and CNN.

Without being debriefed, the soldiers were bombarded with questions by the reporters. "I got nauseous and vomited," Hernandez confessed. "They brought me a bag and I turned around, and Hudson was also vomiting."

Escorted by two Marines, Hernandez and crew were flown to a tent trauma hospital. There, they would be treated by an Army doctor. As a turf scuffle broke out between the Marine Corporals assigned to the former POWs and the doctor, ranks clashed. The ex-captives were finally handed over to a Colonel and were treated.

Afterwards, the soldiers were flown in a Blackhawk helicopter to a Kuwaiti hospital where they were greeted by a swarm of doctors and officers. "We told them we were hungry and they took us to a room," Hernandez remembered. "There were tables full of food; healthy looking food, main course chicken and rice. They asked us, 'What do you guys want? We can make you anything.' We said we want Burger King, pizza, and sodas. And they started laughing."

A Kuwaiti soldier volunteered to go on a Burger King run for the group. Satisfied, the soldiers were finally given phones to use. Calling home, where Army soldiers were standing by his parents, Hernandez talked to his mother.

"She was crying and so was I," Hernandez recalled, "and everything was OK. We talked for a short time in Spanish. She asked what happened. I told her I got shot in the arm but I was fine. We spent four days there and we had someone assigned to us all the time."

Chapter Twenty-Five

Story of Our Lost Comrades

Debriefed, the soldiers told their entire story to military personnel. There they learned that Jessica Lynch had been rescued.

"We were all excited because we believed she was dead," Hernandez remembered. "That was great news to know she was alive and back home safe. Then, they told us what happened the day of our capture. We asked them who died and they brought us a list. When they read the list, we were alone with one female officer and it was pretty sad. We did know of some but now we knew all the names."

Afterwards, the military had prepared a surprise for the freed soldiers. They had brought one friend to spend a few days with each of the former captives. For Hernandez, they brought his roommate from the 507th, Specialist Nicholas Petterson.

"We talked a lot, and it was very difficult to sleep," Hernandez recalled. "We were not allowed to leave so we hung out. They would bring us food, and yes, I did enjoy my first shower after 21 days! It felt good."

One of the pilot's friends brought Young his guitar and that evening the group sat on the balcony together, often waving at the Muslim nurses below. "They looked very young and single," Hernandez recalled with a smile. "We flirted back and forth by waving."

Young began playing his newfound guitar and the group began singing, "Outside" by the band Staind.

"When we were singing the song, I was thinking back, and I would get all sentimental," Hernandez mused.

The next four days were spent seeing different doctors. Not free to move as they pleased, Hernandez recalled that by this point the group had become very close.

Hernandez noted that exactly one year later, the friend of Williams who had come to visit the just freed POW had been shot down in Iraq.

"Williams told us later that he was a pallbearer at his friend's funeral," Hernandez said sadly. "It was important to be there for his friend."

Chapter Twenty-Six

Finally Safe

An ambulance took Hernandez and the other soldiers to the airport where they boarded a C-17 Jumbo jet en route to Germany. Hernandez sat on a "catlike bench" on the side of the plane and strapped his seatbelt on. He and his friends glanced around the plane and were deeply saddened by what they saw. Although their safety was secure, death hovered around them.

"I looked around me," Hernandez recalled, "and the plane was full of soldiers on stretchers. They were in really bad shape. The majority of them did not have arms, and some of them were missing legs.

"These poor soldiers," he continued. "Nurses were taking care of them, checking IV's, and we were all very quiet.

"They were right in front of us, dying. One soldier looked like he may be blind. They were in serious condition."

Chapter Twenty-Seven

Debriefed by Special Forces

When the aircraft landed in Germany, the wounded soldiers were taken off the plane first and the ex-POWs followed. Escorted to a separate bus with MP's watching, they were going to be debriefed by Special Forces.

"I spent a few hours telling them the whole story," Hernandez said. "The entire thing was recorded."

Spending the night in a special facility, Hernandez explained that surprisingly, he could not fall asleep. "It was so peaceful and silent. I was looking at the walls. It felt weird not to be around war.

"I walked to the main room and all my friends were there. None of us slept a wink that first night."

The next few days, the American soldiers spent their time watching television. CNN was running their story "round the clock." However, Hernandez and his peers were ordered not to say anything publicly. On the fourth day, the soldiers, still ordered to remain silent, faced the media for the first time.

"We walked out onto a balcony where a microphone was set up," Hernandez recalled. "We looked down and saw a bunch of cameras and reporters. Williams went up to the podium and thanked everyone for their prayers."

"We are safe now," Williams said.

The soldiers waved to everyone still trying to grasp the fact that they were out of harm's way. What was once surreal became the norm and vice-versa. Now, it was a strange thing to not have to look over your shoulder and pray for your own survival. Freedom was suddenly a luxury and Hernandez knew that he had changed from the experience. The world around him would never look the same.

Chapter Twenty-Eight

Where's Bush?

Anxious to return States side, the freed soldiers were taken to a German airport where the Air Force would fly them back home on a C-17. "We were the only passengers onboard except for the flight crew," Hernandez recalled. "We took pictures with all of them. They told us we could go to the cabin and talk with the pilots. So, we took turns and I talked to both pilots while in cruise control."

A fan of the Red Hot Chili Peppers, Hernandez was handed a laptop and headphones, listening to the band's latest release while he gazed out the windows at the passing clouds.

"As I listened to the music," Hernandez reflected, "I started remembering all my friends who died. And now I was going home but my friends didn't make it. I remember before we left, Estrella told me that when we got back we would go on a trip with our girlfriends. He was planning on getting married when he returned but now he was not coming home. I was thinking of this and I was sad, yet, I was happy I made it out alive. I had mixed emotions."

Back in his seat, the group sat together, talking and relaxing as they flew back to Fort Bliss. Before landing, the former POWs were told what to expect when they arrived home. They were informed a crowd of nearly 2,000 people, which included their families, would be waiting to welcome them home. And according to rumor, the President of the United States would be there to greet them, as well.

"When we were taxied in, they asked Hudson and Miller to look out a small window and they were holding an American Flag," Hernandez noted. "They looked cool and that photo became a huge deal in all the newspapers. So, we came out of the plane and all the families were there. We hugged, cried and talked for a few minutes."

The freed pilots, Williams and Young, were flown to Fort Hood where they met President George W. Bush.

"We found out they met the President," Hernandez

disappointedly said. "We would have loved to have met him, too. We had a nice ceremony and it was a big deal but I wish the President would have come to see us."

At Fort Bliss, the soldiers were assigned to the hospital for a two-week stay of checkups and mental evaluations. When it was time to return home, Hernandez flew first class. On his flight, the pilot announced there was a POW onboard and all the passengers applauded. "That felt pretty good," Hernandez confessed.

At the McAllen Airport, Hernandez was greeted by the mayors of McAllen, Alton and his hometown of Mission, Texas. "My family was also there," Hernandez remembered, "and some school kids started singing to me. That was pretty cool. I was nervous and not sure what to say. They told me just to say thank you."

At an afternoon press conference, the returning local hero was awarded various plaques and a medal. "I told everyone thanks and we walked out, and they had a limousine for me with a police escort," Hernandez said in disbelief.

With the media camped out in front of his house, Hernandez was taken to another location to lay low. While watching the TV, he saw the press waiting at his home. "That was funny," Hernandez pointed out. "I could hear them say, 'ex-POW Edgar Hernandez will be home soon. He just left the airport and is on his way here.' There were cars driving up and down my street, waving flags. It was a pretty big deal."

Initially, life back home consisted of just spending time with family. But with his newfound fame, and the appreciation from the townspeople, Hernandez enjoyed numerous complimentary meals, including lunch with the mayor. He even threw out the opening pitch at a local baseball game.

May 3, 2003, was declared 'Edgar Hernandez Day' and a parade was organized in his honor. "I was waving at everyone," Hernandez recalled. Afterwards, a rally with 6,000 people cheered Hernandez on. A nervous and grateful soldier thanked the well-wishers.

Chapter Twenty-Nine

Top Soldier in America

On May 31, 2003, Hernandez returned to El Paso, Texas. Eager to live his life to the fullest, it dawned on him that serving his country meant everything to him. Therefore, on July 25, 2003, Hernandez re-enlisted in the Army for four more years.

"I loved the feeling of serving my country," the young soldier stated. "My family thought I was crazy and became very angry when they discovered what I was doing.

When Mama Hernandez heard this, she called her son very upset. She almost lost him once and the thought of going through the great emotional despair that soldier's families endure a second time was too much to bear. However, Hernandez assured her that while the military didn't guarantee he would not return to Iraq, there was a rule in place regarding POWs being sent back to combat.

"When I went to the recruiter center and signed up," Hernandez recalled, "they were all excited and told me that I could choose to do something that was different and safe.

"I chose to be a dental assistant for the U.S. Army and I asked to be stationed at Sam Houston military base in San Antonio. I was treated like a celebrity, and at first it was fun. Everyone was friendly to me and they even asked for autographs. They took pictures of me and I did many interviews for local TV stations and some Spanish language TV stations."

Things eventually slowed down for Hernandez and with the support of his fellow POWs, he was able to keep both feet firmly on the ground. Williams and Hernandez became good friends.

"I looked up to him," Hernandez said. "He even kept his promise and took me flying."

After their escape, Williams went on to become a helicopter pilot instructor where he was stationed in Fort

Rucker, Alabama. Meanwhile, Hernandez put all of his energy into becoming the best soldier possible. Aside from Williams, another mentor of his was Staff Sergeant Omar Mascarena.

"Mascarena was the best non-commissioned officer in America and in Europe," explained Hernandez. "He competed for many years and received The Sergeant Audie Murphy Medal of Excellence, which is the most prestigious board in the Army."

Hernandez aspired to be just like Mascarena and worked hard at living up to his mentor's elite reputation. After competing for Soldier of the Month, Soldier of the Quarter and Soldier of the Year, and winning all three prizes while simultaneously attending college, Hernandez moved on to the regional competition where he represented Texas.

"There were seven of us from different parts of the South," Hernandez noted.

With a helpful push from Mascarena, Hernandez climbed high on the ladder and continued to strive for more each day. Although his capture in Iraq was a living nightmare, it enabled him to fearlessly pursue goals that once seemed unattainable. "Can't" no longer exists in Hernandez's vocabulary.

Chapter Thirty

To Protect and Serve

After deciding it was time to get out of the military, Hernandez ended his active duty career in May 2007. Eager to begin civilian life, the now 26-year-old was looking forward to life as a police officer.

"I was at home one day and I got a call from Detective Roy Padilla, Hernandez recalled. "He asked if I wanted to become an officer and I said, 'Of course.'"

As a favor, Hernandez went to the local baseball stadium

and gave a motivational speech to a group of teenagers. "In my uniform, I spoke to them about staying in school and not doing drugs."

Next, Detective Padilla invited Hernandez to lunch with the Chief of Police. The former soldier was on the fast-track to the academy. Having passed a series of tests to gain admission to the police department, the only remaining exam was the physical test. With a sprained ankle wrapped in tape, Hernandez demonstrated how tough he was by completing the obstacle course.

Passing the Pharr police entrance exam, Hernandez was now one of seven candidates, out of an original 89, to get to the Police Academy. A word of advice that Hernandez shares to prospective candidates is to realize that their permanent record is indeed permanent, at least when being considered for law enforcement.

"The background check disqualifies many people because they think if they did something as a juvenile it would not show up, but it does," Hernandez said. "They will disqualify you."

In the Academy for just two weeks, the Hernandez family was stricken by a deep blow when Edgar's father suffered a stroke. "It was so unexpected and soon after, he past away," the loving son remembered. "He was young, only 62-years-old and very healthy. It caught us by surprise. He was on life-support but never recovered from the initial heart attack. It was difficult. I am the oldest and my mom took it very hard. We all suffered from his loss but he is resting in peace today. He was buried at Garden of Angels cemetery in Mission, Texas on October 2, 2007.

Having graduated from the academy, Hernandez, along with six of his classmates, traveled to Austin to take the State Police Exam. The group scored the highest marks in the state. "Our chief was very proud of us," Hernandez boasted. "This academy has become kind of famous."

With the second highest score to his credit, Hernandez has made quite a reputation for himself. "Today, they kid me about my score here at the Pharr Police Department."

On February 13, 2008, before family and friends and high-ranking officers from Pharr, Hernandez graduated from the Academy. "I felt very proud to be wearing the Police uniform for the first time," the former POW reflects. "Life is pretty good."

POWs rescued April 20, 2003
Photos courtesy of Edgar's friends

Moments after rescue by U.S. Marines

Hernandez and Hudson
on flight to El Paso, Texas from Germany

POWs rescued April 20, 2003
in happier times; group photo

Edgar Hernandez at Biggs Army Airfield,
El Paso, Texas April 2003

Diaz, Friend, Peterson and Hernandez

Welcome Home Edgar Hernandez

Mom and Dad, may he rest in peace

Edgar Hernandez Day Parade
Mission, Texas 2003

Edgar Hernandez waving at crowd
with parents

Un Heroe

Un heroe, una persona, que supera
Todo lo que quiera,
Un heroe de guerra va a pelear por su nacion
Como marcando el principio de toda relacion,
Va luchando, va peleando,
Pero tambien va liberando,
Asi como una cancion que es un canto
Y que a todas las personas les gusta tanto,
El heroe es valiente,
Y a el lo apoya la gente,
Un heroe, Edgar Hernandez,
Que fue liberando a muchas ciudades,
Lo capturaron y lo secuestraron,
Pero al ultimo lo liberaron,
Y todas las personas lo festejaron.

Salvador Blas Torres

McAllen City Commissioners Ric Godinez and Aida Ramirez presented Edgar with a key to the city.

Mr. Salvador Vela introduced Edgar and invited everyone to the May 3, 2003, Alton celebration in Edgar's honor. A full day will be dedicated to Edgar beginning with a parade.

Mr. Ricardo Cortez, former P.O.W. and now McAllen resident was in attendance, showing his support to the Hernández family.

Former POW Ricardo Cortez

CWO3 David Williams
close friend and former POW

Hernandez with Texas Governor Rick Perry

McAllen City Commissioners
Ric Godinez and Aida Ramirez
presented Edgar with a key
to the city.

Edgar with wife Yuliana Gonzalez Hernandez
married November 20, 2007

Dad with and Edgar Jr and
step son David Michael

David Michael, dog Tito and Edgar

Edgar age two, David Michael, Edgar Jr.

Family at Edgar's wedding: brother Joel, mother-in-law Zoraida Fernandez, Edgar, wife Yulicana, David Michael, Maria De La Luz (Edgar's mom), sister-in-law Zoraida II, brother-in-law David, sister-in-law Aby Gonzalez with daughter Ezra

Edgar with his 2008 Ford Mustang

Edgar's wife Yulicana Gonzalez Hernandez
and family

Chapter Thirty-One

Reflection

Having survived as a Prisoner of War in Iraq, Hernandez, reflecting on his harrowing experience, has formed a personnel perspective on war:

Life has not been the same since my return home. I caught myself comparing how they live in Iraq and how we live here in the States. It feels like many people take freedom for granted.

I just returned from a country that has been fighting for its freedom for hundreds of years. It is such a poor country and many people are barely surviving day-to-day.

What happened to me wasn't like the movies because it is real. You lose friends, and engage in real firefights. I know war is not a good thing but I feel patriotic and part of the team that protects America. Joining our military is a big commitment so I feel everyone who serves is a hero.

Epilogue

Reaction from Home – Captured

Upon the news of Hernandez's capture, his family back in Texas was shocked as their world spun out of control. The headline in the local newspaper read: Edgar Hernandez From Texas Has Been Captured.

Monica Hernandez, Sister
I first heard of my brother's capture on TV. I saw the news and they showed his face and said he had been captured. When I called home, the news crews had arrived there already. I raced over there and we spent a lot of time praying as a family for his

safe return.

Marco Antonio Hernandez, Brother

I was 17 in San Marcos, Texas, studying in a computer trade school when my brother was captured. My Mom called me at 6AM saying Edgar is a POW in Iraq. I was in shock and denial at first. I did not want to believe her.

I drove home, which was a six-hour drive, and stayed there the entire time he was missing. It was crazy at home. So many people were coming to our door.

My dad would tell us to "stay strong." He'd say, "It was God's will and things would turn out OK."

Joel Alejandro Hernandez, Brother

I was 18 and planning on joining the military and Edgar told me I should wait a year before joining because he was being deployed to Iraq and there was going to be a war. He said, 'I know you want to join the military but we're getting deployed to Iraq and a lot of soldiers and going. I don't think it is a good idea for both of us to be in the military during a war.' It would be very difficult on our mom.

That day I woke up at 7AM to go to work. My dad was watching the news and said that the 507th Maintenance Company stationed in El Paso, Texas had been ambushed and five members were captured and many killed. He said that among the captured, was a Hispanic male around 21-years-old. As soon as I heard that I had a bad feeling and hoped it was not my brother.

I went to work thinking about this the whole time. When it was confirmed that it was him, I felt pretty devastated. Always growing up, my brother was a little quite, not very aggressive and kind of shy. So, it was hard to know that he was in that situation, and I was expecting the worst. I took off from work early, and as soon as I got home we got a call from the military. They confirmed that Edgar was missing. Right after that, we got bombarded with phone calls from news agencies and newspapers.

A military vehicle then drove up with the Sheriff. They walked in the house and explained the situation. One thing that stood out and kind of shocked me was they walked in with a portfolio, opened it up and took out some papers and read off: 'Specialist Hernandez is missing in action. We do not know if he is dead or alive but we know that he is missing. We are trying to our best to find these soldiers.'

What was weird to me is that they did not have a clue on his condition. Knowing Iraq and their desire to kill Americans, we though the worst. My mom was freaking out. That evening, on a Mexican news station, we saw my brother. He was bleeding from his face. I could tell he was very weak; they had to help him up. If they would not have patched up his wounds, he would have bled to death.

Maria De La Luz Hernandez, Mother

When we heard about his capture, I saw it first on TV. I saw him and I knew it was my son and my husband kept telling me it couldn't be our Edgar. I was very sure it was him. I was crying and my husband kept trying to console me. That's when a Police Officer called and wanted our address. Soon after, they arrived at the door.

I would call the Red Cross and who ever else I could call, and once I spoke to a Senator in Washington DC. She told us that they found the uniforms full of blood but believed they were alive. She concluded by assuring us that they are searching for the POWs.

Sergeant Abraham Hernandez, Cousin Second Infantry Division, Fort Luis, WA

I was stationed in Fort Drum, New York with the 10th Mountain Division, getting ready to deploy to Afghanistan and we were about three weeks out from our deployment. My mom called and told me to turn on the news and that my cousin Edgar was a POW in Iraq. I didn't want to believe her. I was in shock and sure enough, I turned on the news and they were talking about the POWs. They showed Edgar on the TV and that confirmed the news for me.

My first thoughts were, 'I want to go over there and do every-thing I can as a soldier to bring him home.' I felt boxed in because I could not do anything.

Epilogue

Reaction from Home – Rescued

As news of Hernandez's rescue made its way around the globe, family members were overwrought with joy.

Monica Hernandez, Sister
When he was rescued, it was great news! I was with the family and when we heard, we were so happy.

Marco Antonio Hernandez, Brother
When he was rescued, we heard there was one Hispanic soldier and we knew it was him. It was a great feeling to know he was

safe and everyone was there to support us with their friendship.

When Edgar was rescued, Home Depot came to Mom's house and did some repairs, which was cool.

Richard Cortez, Mayor of McAllen, Texas
Any time you hear good news about servicemen who are POW or a rescue, it is great for everyone, especially the family, who has been suffering through the ordeal. I think highly of Edgar on how he handled himself in a time of crisis and after his release from captivity. He exemplifies how valuable American servicemen and women are to our country.

Mission, Texas is our neighbor city but it is like home to us and we care very much about Mission and its citizens. It pleases me to hear that he is back at home and I want to thank him for his service to our country and wish him all the success in his career in law enforcement.

Salvador Vela, Mayor of Alton, Texas
Edgar Hernandez was a Prisoner of War and I believe his rescue was truly a miracle. We would gather at the local churches and at the elementary school and pray for his safe return. When we heard the Marines had gone in and rescued them, we were very excited and very grateful our prayers were answered.

We had a great parade for him here in Alton. We have a dedicated Edgar Hernandez Day here in the city. He is a true hero. All the local mayors were here and you should have seen the crowds. We are very proud of Edgar. He was overseas serving our country to protect our freedom.

Joel Alejandro Hernandez, Brother

On the day of the rescue, we heard from the military and the news stations. There was a phone call that they had rescued the POWs and then we saw the soldiers on TV. He looked a lot better from the first time we saw him. It was a huge relief to the whole family that he was safe.

I have always supported my brother in the career he has chosen. He is a military man. Growing up, we would always share our dreams and support each other. We are a close family.

Maria De La Luz Hernandez, Mother

One day we heard on the news that they had rescued the POWs and they were safe. They were not 100% positive on the first news reports but soon after, it was confirmed. It was a great moment and we were all very happy and jubilant about the news. Within hours, we saw his picture on TV as he was walking towards the helicopter. It was great to see him. After that, the house was full of people. That evening, we heard from Edgar by phone and he said he was safe and doing well.

Within a couple of weeks, he arrived in El Paso. He was finally back and we could hug him and see he was safe. I am very proud of my son. He re-enlisted soon after he returned from Iraq. It was his decision again. But after another four years, Edgar is back and home with his family for good.

Edgar remembering our fallen soldiers

Repatriation Of POWs, from left:
Shoshana Johnson, Joe Hudson, Edgar, former POW
Robert Mitchelle, David Williams, Patrick Miller and
James Riley

Cadets swearing-in ceremony

With friend Roy Padilla

With Chief Villescas

Instructor Castaneda, Chief Villescas, Cadets: Jesse Lopez, Herald Gomez, Henry Vargas, Jerry Garza, Edgar, Instructor Gonzales, Assistant Chief Gonzalez, and Assistant Chief Perez

To Protect and Serve, Pharr, Texas

Edgar Hernandez – June 14, 2003
Texas Rangers vs. Florida Marlins
(AP Images / Tim Sharp)

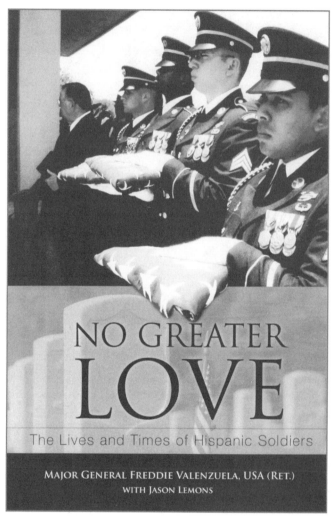

NO GREATER LOVE

The Lives and Times of Hispanic Soldiers

MAJOR GENERAL FREDDIE VALENZUELA, USA (RET.)
WITH JASON LEMONS

For information on
No Greater Love:
The Lives and Times of Hispanic Soldiers
Visit:
SupportFallenSoldiers.com
SupportAtRiskChildren.com

Honoring Forgotten Heroes
Hispanics In American Wars

For more information
Visit:
HonoringForgottenHeroes.com
EdgarHernandezMyStory.com

Visit
former POW Edgar Hernandez at:

EdgarHernandezMyStory.com

Visit
Major General Alfred Valenzuela at:

SupportFallenSoldiers.com
SupportAtRiskChildren.com

Visit us at:

HonoringForgottenHeroes.com

Contact us at:

OceanBreezeBooks@yahoo.com